The ABC's of
Elder Law & Estate Planning

DAVID WINGATE

Copyright © 2016 David Wingate.

All rights reserved. No part of this book may be reproduced, stored, or transmitted by any means—whether auditory, graphic, mechanical, or electronic—without written permission of both publisher and author, except in the case of brief excerpts used in critical articles and reviews. Unauthorized reproduction of any part of this work is illegal and is punishable by law.

ISBN: 978-1-4834-4783-4 (sc)
ISBN: 978-1-4834-4784-1 (e)

Because of the dynamic nature of the Internet, any web addresses or links contained in this book may have changed since publication and may no longer be valid. The views expressed in this work are solely those of the author and do not necessarily reflect the views of the publisher, and the publisher hereby disclaims any responsibility for them.

Any people depicted in stock imagery provided by Thinkstock are models, and such images are being used for illustrative purposes only. Certain stock imagery © Thinkstock.

Lulu Publishing Services rev. date: 03/17/2016

CONTENTS

Introduction vii

A: Annuity 1
B: Bypass Trust 3
C: Codicil 5
D: Durable Power of Attorney 6
E. End of Life Care 9
F. Financing Long Term Care 12
G. Guardianship 16
H. Health Care Agent 19
I. Irrevocable Trust 23
J. Joint Tenancy 27
K. Korean War Veterans 30
L. Long-Term Care Insurance 32
M. Medicare & Medicaid 37
N. Nursing Home 48
O. Ombudsman 51
P. Probate 54
Q. Qualification for Medicaid 57
R. Revocable Living Trust 61
S. Supplemental (Special) Needs Trust 63
T. Transferring Assets to Qualify for Medicaid 67
U. Undue Influence 70
V. Vehicles 76
W. Will 79
X. X Out Your Issues 81
Y. Young Children 84
Z. Is the End 85

About David Wingate 87

INTRODUCTION

Planning strategies, we hope, will increase the vitality of your loved ones and provide comfort and relief to you. Our goal is that you or your a loved one live comfortably, secure and be as independent as possible. We want to enhance your quality of life and give you peace of mind. You may need some guidance and support through this aging process, and we hope to help you with this book. Also, we hope to encourage you to plan, strategize and manage you or your loved ones care, finances and legal issues utilizing all the services and resources available to you in your community.

We have seen the devastating effects that the lack of planning can have on a family, or your loved one entering into a nursing home. Consequently, we advise you to take action before a crisis hits you or your family. **Good care is costly, but inadequate planning and care is catastrophic.**

Therefore, whether you reside at home, an independent or assisted living facility or a nursing home, we hope that this book will help you charter those waters so you can maintain a quality of life.

A: ANNUITY

Although there are many types of annuities, we use a Medicaid compliant annuity for asset protection planning, i.e. protecting your assets from the nursing home. An annuity is simply an agreement by an insurance company to pay a certain amount of money to a specified person for a predetermined period of time.

Annuities can be purchased by writing a check to the insurance company, and completing the contract. With the implementation of the Deficit Reduction Act of 2005 ("DRA") in February 2005, to be Medicaid complaint, the annuity must:

- Be irrevocable and non-assignable;
- Be actuarially sound;
- Provide for payments in equal amounts, with no deferral and no balloon payment; and
- Name the State Medicaid agency as the beneficiary, to the extent that Medical Assistance benefits were provided to institutionalized individual.

What does this mean? Basically, the Medicaid compliant annuity is designed to convert assets into an income stream over a fixed period of time. Thus, with the assets eliminated, the Medicaid applicant becomes eligible for Medicaid benefits.

Division of assets is the name commonly used for the Spousal Impoverishment provision of the Medicare Catastrophic Act of 1988. It applies only to married couples. The intent of the law was to change the eligibility requirements for Medicaid in situations where one spouse needs nursing home care, while the other spouse remains in the community (i.e. at home or in an assisted living facility). Since then, changes in the law have now allowed spouses who are at home to sometimes qualify for Medicaid assistance for certain home and community-based services.

Basically, in a division of assets, a couple gathers all of their assets. Exempt assets, such as the home, one vehicle, and so on are not counted. The non-exempt assets, such as checking and saving accounts, CD's, IRA's, Whole Life Insurance etc. are then divided in two, with the community (or at home) spouse allowed to keep one-half of all of the countable assets, up to a maximum of $119,220 (2016). The other one-half of the assets must then be "spent down."

For example, a married couple has $100,000 in countable assets. The well spouse, or community spouse, is able to keep one-half of those assets (i.e. $50,000 in this example) and the ill spouse will have to "spend down" basically $48,000 and keep his or her $2,000, to qualify for Medicaid. To qualify for Medicaid the ill spouse must have assets below $2,500. In lieu of paying the $48,000 to the nursing home, transfer the $48,000 to an insurance company, for the purchase of a Medicaid friendly annuity, and the ill spouse will qualify for Medicaid. The $48,000 will then be paid to the community spouse, in monthly payments, over a fixed period of time (e.g. 48 months x $1,000 = $48,000.) Consequently, all the money is returned to the community spouse.

We have had a number clients utilize this strategy. They are thrilled to save money, for their own use, rather than to pay for the nursing home.

B: BYPASS TRUST

A bypass trust is a trust, established to utilize the estate tax exclusion amount under 26 U.S. Code 2010. The trust is designed to provide for your surviving spouse (when you die), but _not_ be included in the surviving spouse's estate at their death.

The basics of the bypass trust – you create your bypass trust that will take effect when you die. You name your spouse as the beneficiary of the trust. Consequently, you fund the trust with real property i.e. your home; investments; and savings accounts, etc. Upon your death, no estate tax will be due.

The principal purpose of the bypass trust is to give the surviving spouse access to the trust property, but to avoid taxation of the trust property in the estate of the surviving spouse. Thus, the more value held in the bypass trust, the less taxes will be paid at your spouses' death.

Your spouse has only those rights to the trust property outlined in the trust i.e. receiving trust income, use of real property, and spend the trust property on specific needs – health, education, maintenance, and support, etc.

Upon the death of your surviving spouse, the surviving spouse does not own any of the trust property. Thus, the trust property is not part of your surviving spouse's estate, so no estate taxes are due.

Then the remaining trust property shall be distributed to named contingent beneficiaries, usually, your children.

However, with the Federal Estate Tax, currently at $5.45 million (2016) most people do not have to worry about paying Federal Estate Tax. Consequently, the bypass trust is redundant. However, you should utilize the Revocable and Irrevocable Trusts, to avoid Probate, and protect their assets from the nursing home.

C: CODICIL

You have already prepared a Will, but now, you desire to amend your existing Will. Essentially, there are two ways to amend your Will:

- Prepare a codicil to the Will; or
- Prepare a new Will and thus revoke the old Will.

A codicil is a legal document that makes changes to a Will that has already been drafted, signed and witnessed. Like the Will, a codicil must be typed, signed, dated and witnessed.

For example: Codicil to Will of the Cowardly Lion

- Delete paragraph 1 and add in its place:
- I leave three thousand ($3,000) dollars to the Tin Man.
- I leave my Medal of Courage to the Scarecrow
- In all other respects, I reaffirm my Will dated .....

    Signed: The Cowardly Lion
    Witness: Dorothy
    Witness: The Wizard of Oz

    Notary: Glenda, the Good Witch of the North

Codicils were used frequently, years ago to avoid the cost and expense of retyping a new Will. However, today, especially with computers, it is usually easier to prepare a new Will rather than prepare the codicil.

D: DURABLE POWER OF ATTORNEY

A Durable Power of Attorney is a legal document by which you designate another person (i.e. spouse) as your attorney-in-fact ("agent") to handle your financial affairs.

If you become unable to manage your financial affairs and you failed to prepare a Durable Power of Attorney, then your spouse, family or somebody else will have to file for Guardianship. The Guardianship proceeding is time consuming and very expensive. Therefore, the Durable Power of Attorney is a means to avoid the necessity of a court appointed Guardian of the Property.

A Durable Power of Attorney can take effect:

- Immediately, or
- Springing.

Which one you choose depends on when you desire your Durable Power of Attorney to take effect. If you require your agent to help you with your finances "Immediately" – then make the Durable Power of Attorney effective upon signing. Consequently, your agent can perform such actions, like pay your insurance or mortgage bills, write checks, make deposits into your bank accounts, etc.

However, if you want to remain in control of your financial affairs until you are declared incompetent, by two physicians, then your Durable Power of Attorney should be executed as a "springing" power of attorney.

I prefer a Durable Power of Attorney to be effective immediately rather when you are declared incompetent. Until you are declared incompetent, by two physicians, then you, technically do not have an agent to work for you. Therefore, a financial institution i.e. bank will not recognize the agent until they receive proof that you have been declared incompetent, by two physicians, which can be time consuming and problematic. Consequently, your affairs may be delayed or not be completed depending on the circumstances.

The selection of an agent is extremely important. You must be confident that the selected person is trustworthy, responsible and to some degree be financially knowledgeable. It is always advisable to name at least one successor agent.

I suggest that you should give your agent broad powers over your finances to:

- Buy or sell your home;
- Purchase or sell household goods, such furniture, silverware, clothing, etc;
- Deal with you financial advisor to buy or sell stocks or bonds, commodities and options;
- Perform transactions at your bank e.g. writing checks, making deposits or withdrawals;
- Manage your business affairs, if you own a business;
- Buy or sell insurance and annuity products;
- Act for you in court or hire an attorney to represent your interests;
- Apply and receive Government benefits from Social Security, Medicare, VA and/or Medicaid etc;
- Distribute Gifts – this is very important to have to protect your assets from the nursing home;
- Administer your IRA, 401K, Pension or other retirement accounts; and
- Claim or disclaim inherited property.

After you have signed your Durable Power of Attorney (if effective immediately) your document will take effect. Your agent will need a

David Wingate

copy to act on your behalf. I also recommend that you provide your bank, financial advisor or other institutions copies of your Durable Power of Attorney.

Also, your Durable Power of Attorney can be modified, at any time, provided you are not dead or legally incompetent.

Most people, regrettably, do not have Durable Powers of Attorney, as they believe they are too young to need one, or that something is not going to happen to them. Many years ago a client, in her late thirties, came to our office, for the preparation of a Durable Power of Attorney. She became busy, and never made time to sign the document. Unfortunately, she was in a car accident and in a coma for a number of months. Since she did not have a Durable Power of Attorney, nobody could handle her financial affairs, until a costly and time consuming Guardianship was completed.

E. END OF LIFE CARE

How can you make sure that your wishes are obeyed if you become incapable of making decisions at the end of your life? With an Advance Directive (Living Will), you can set forth your end of life instructions. The use of life sustaining medical equipment, over the last few years, has fostered distress that our lives may be artificially prolonged against our wishes. The United States Supreme Court has held that every person has the constitutional right to control his or her medical treatment – even if those wishes are directly opposed by the patient's family. (Cruzan Vs. Director, Missouri Department of Health, 497 U.S. 261 (1990)).

Consequently, to control your own medical treatment, you must create an Advance Directive. This directive can thus alleviate your fears, if you are in a vegetative state, terminal or end stage condition, about receiving unwanted medical treatment at the end of your life. Additionally, this directive eases the pain and decisions for family members, from making heartbreaking decision about the treatment or lack thereof that you desire.

The Advance Directive (Living Will) is a legal document in which you state your wishes about life support, withdrawal of treatment and comfort care.

Medical care during the end of life stages can be traumatic, for both you and your family. Sometimes, the hospital and nursing home are more concerned about keeping you alive, to make money rather taking your wishes into consideration. Consequently, we advocate for the use of Hospice.

Hospice provides care designed for people who have less than six months to live or a failure to thrive. Failure to thrive is most commonly seen in the frail elderly who may not have one specific terminal illness, but may have one or more chronic illness. They often have poor appetite, loss of weight, increased fatigue and a progressive functional decline. Thus they may be eligible for the services provided by the Medicare Hospice Benefit under the diagnosis of failure to thrive.

Hospice is an approach to enhance your quality of life by pain management and symptom relief, while addressing your emotional, and your family's social and spiritual needs. Hospice lets you share the end of life experience with dignity. In most cases you can stay at home. However, Hospice care can be provided at an Assisted Living Facility or Nursing Home. Hospice team members and volunteers are available to provide services, including but not limited to:

- Pain and symptoms management;
- Assistance with emotional, psychological, social and spiritual needs;
- Administer drugs, medical supplies and equipment;
- Training for family caregivers; and
- Bereavement counseling.

Medicare pays most of the Hospice cost. For eligibility, you must be covered by Medicare Part A, and have a physician's certificate stating that your life expectancy is less than six months. To enroll in Hospice, you must sign a statement electing Hospice benefits. This election shifts the course of treatment from curative to palliative care i.e. treating pain not the disease.

In addition to Medicare, Medicaid and most private health insurance companies also offer Hospice coverage. Hospice should be considered by everyone who is nearing the end of life.

We have had a number of clients return to our office to thank us for the preparation of the Advance Directive. They stated that everything went smoothly because they had all the necessary paperwork done. There are plenty of horror stories about family members fighting, not talking to each other, and not respecting the wishes of their loved ones at end of life because the Advance Directive was not prepared. The most notable case involved Terri Schiavo. The Terri Schiavo case was a legal battle over an end-of-life decision. Schiavo's husband argued that she did not want to prolong her life in a vegetative state, and thus elected to remove her feeding tube. However, Schiavo's parents argued in favor of continuing artificial nutrition and hydration. After, all the legal challenges offered by her parents, which caused a seven-year delay, Schiavo's feeding tube was finally removed. Thus, to avoid all this mess we highly recommend you prepare and sign an Advance Directive (Living Will).

F. FINANCING LONG TERM CARE

Most people desire to stay at home, while receiving long term care to maintain their independence. However, this independence can be a burden on your family. Before any long term care decisions are made, you must involve all of your family to discuss if your needs can be met by family members and/or outside care. You may need the following type of care:

- Weekly assistance;
- Daily assistance;
- 24/7 care;
- Driving to doctors, shops and social; or
- Housekeeping and maintenance.

Depending on the activities requested, the cost of long term care can vary from minor to prohibitively expensive. Homecare can be less expensive than residential care if only needed on a limited basis. But, comprehensive home care if utilized can exceed residential care. Residential facilities – independent living, assisted living facilities and nursing homes greatly vary in cost. We have seen costs for independent living facilities start at three thousand dollars per month, depending on location and activities. An assisted living facility can cost between five thousand and eight thousand dollars per month and nursing homes can cost over ten thousand dollars per month, depending on your location.

Unfortunately, Medicare and Medicaid do not pay for home or assisted living facility care. (Maryland has a limited waiver program).

Basically, Medicare will only pay for a limited amount of rehabilitative nursing home care and Medicaid only pays for long term nursing home care, if and when, you qualify for Medicaid. Therefore, you need to pay privately or have an insurance company pay, with long term care insurance, if you require home or assisted living care.

Because you pay home care out of your own pocket, we advise you to interview at least two home care companies. Before signing up with a home care company, review how the company will bill you to ensure that the company will not include charges for services you don't desire or need. Always, review the invoice against the timesheets provided. Also, review the company's invoice against the estimate they provided you to ensure you are obtaining everything you contracted for.

Most independent and assisted living facilities are rented monthly, not purchased. Obviously, the rent depends on the location of the facility, the type of facility, the size of the living space, and the amenities of the facilities. As with any rental facilities, each year the rent increases. Also, most facilities charge fees in addition to rent i.e. entrance fee, fees for services not included in the basic rent, transportation, personal care beyond the standard level of care, and extra housekeeping services, etc.

The more you pay, you would think leads to improved quality of care. However, this is not necessarily the case with nursing home facilities. Many nursing home facilities have expensive medical equipment and staff. However, most residents will not require the utilization of the expensive medical equipment but will have to pay for it, in their rent. For most people the cost of care in a nursing home will deplete their assets. Subsequently, Medicaid will pay for the cost of the nursing home residents' care when they are impoverished.

Reverse Mortgage

You may finance home care costs through a reverse mortgage. A reverse mortgage is a loan against your home paid in a lump sum, monthly, a line of credit, or a combination thereof. If you do not have sufficient income or assets to pay for long term costs at home, and you own your home you may qualify for a reverse mortgage. By utilizing a reverse mortgage, you can convert home equity into cash, thus remaining at home. This loan does not have to be repaid until you die, vacate your home, or sell your home. Although, reverse mortgages appear attractive, they do have some drawbacks, initial costs such as:

- Appraisal fees
- Credit checks
- Closing costs
- Insurance
- Service charges.

Also, there are continuing fees and interest payments each year. Consequently, a reverse mortgage may be more expensive than a conventional loan or line of credit. Consequently, I am typically not a great fan of a reverse mortgage. But, for instance, we had a client with no assets except her home. She was not taking care of herself, not eating properly, nor taking her medications. She was trying to exist on her social security of approximately $1,100 per month, and this was her sole income. A bank refused a line of credit, as her income was too low. Therefore, we suggested she should apply for a reverse mortgage. She obtained the reverse mortgage, and this freed up funds to help pay her prescription drugs, rather than cutting them in half, and purchasing nourishing food. With these funds she is able to stay in her home, and have peace of mind.

Long Term Care Insurance

Another way to finance the cost of long term care is to purchase long term care insurance ("LTCI"). There is no simple answer whether LTCI is the right choice for you. You need to consider the cost paid to the insurance company to see if it's worthwhile to purchase the policy. Like any other insurance policy, let the buyer be aware.

From one insurance company to another, there can be a considerable difference in cost for nearly the same policy. A number of factors may increase the insurance premiums, such as:

- Age when you purchase the policy
- Health history
- Types of care covered
- Where you live
- Inflation protection
- Amount of benefits
- Elimination period
- Length of policy

Almost all basic LTCI policies cover home care, assisted living care and nursing home care. LTCI policies pay a fixed amount of benefits for covered care. Most LTCI policies will not begin paying benefits unless you cannot perform a certain number of "activities of daily living" (ADL). ADL's include:

- Bathing
- Dressing
- Eating
- Toileting
- Walking
- Medication
- Continence

We have a client, in his early sixties, one of his concerns was how to pay for long term care and protect his assets. We had an initial consultation and he retained my services to review his estate planning needs and financial goals i.e. making sure his retirement income and assets would last his lifetime. I helped him set up Durable Powers of Attorneys, Advance Directives, Wills and Trusts to handle any unforeseen "long term crisis" during his life and to ensure any remaining assets are distributed properly when he died. I continue to talk to him regularly about his financial and estate planning goals. He feels that he has control of his life, and has peace of mind.

G. GUARDIANSHIP

The state is deemed to have an interest in the well-being of its citizens. Therefore, guardians are appointed by the court, and are responsible in reporting to the court on the well-being and finances of the disabled person. The court's responsibilities consist of:

- Adjudicating disability;
- Appointing a guardian; and
- Administration of the guardian.

There are two types of guardianship in Maryland:

- Guardian of the property; and
- Guardian of the person.

In order to establish Guardian of the property, the court must establish:

- Mental or physical disability;
- Person has assets or property, or is entitled to benefits;
- The assets etc. require management; and
- The person is unable to manage their affairs.

In order to establish Guardian of the person, a court must determine whether the person lacks capacity to handle his or her affairs, including but not limited to shelter, clothing, health care, food, etc.

Any interested person can file a petition with the court seeking guardianship. The petition requesting guardianship must specify the inability of the person to make or communicate responsible decisions concerning their health and welfare – for person; and an inability to manage their financial affairs – for property.

Additionally, other items required in the petition include:

- Name, age and address of the disabled person;
- Identification of the petitioner and their relationship with the disabled person;
- Why a Guardianship is necessary?
- Statement by a physician stating the disability and whether the person can manage their health and/or financial affairs.

A guardianship hearing is held where each side can put forth arguments why or why not a guardianship should be issued. The judge after hearing testimony enters a decision whether for or against a guardianship. A Guardian of the person will be appointed if the court finds by clear and convincing evidence that the person lacks the capacity to communicate or make responsible decisions concerning his or her person. The power and duty of the Guardian of the person is to exercise care and comfort to the disabled person. This includes:

- Social
- Recreational
- Friendship

The Guardian of the property, must not just simply review and protect the disabled person's property, but must interact with the Guardian of the person to spend the disabled person's assets on the disabled person, as necessary.

The Guardian of the person must file an annual report with the court describing the location, health and assets of the disabled person. The report also states the plan for maintaining the disabled person, and whether the guardianship should be continued or terminated.

David Wingate

If you become unable to manage your financial affairs and you failed to prepare a Power of Attorney, your spouse, family or somebody else will have to file for Guardianship. The Guardianship proceeding is time consuming and very expensive. Therefore, we highly recommend that you prepare and sign a Durable Power of Attorney and an Appointment of a Health Care Agent to avoid the necessity of a court appointed Guardian of the Property and Person.

A few years ago we prepared a Durable Power of Attorney and a Health Care Directive for a client in his early sixties. Fortunately, we prepared these documents as he developed Lewy Body Dementia. Lewy Body Dementia is a devastating form of Dementia. If he had waited any longer he may not have been competent to sign these documents, and his daughter would have had to file a Guardianship. Thankfully, the documents were in place so she avoided the time, effort and cost of filing for the Guardianship.

H. HEALTH CARE AGENT

If your health declines to a stage where you cannot make your own decisions, it is essential that you have another person, your health care agent, be able to make these decisions for you. Similar to the Durable Power of Attorney, the Appointment of the Health Care Agent is a legal document that allows another person to make health care decisions for you, if you are unable to do so.

Consequently, you have someone to advocate for you regarding your health care.

Your health care agent will act on your behalf when you are ill or injured and you cannot express your own health care decisions. Thus, the document will "spring" into effect immediately. If you recover and are able to express your own healthcare decisions, your health care agent's authority will be discontinued.

When choosing a healthcare agent, you must be able to trust that person. Most people choose their spouse, family or a close friend. This position can be challenging and agonizing. Your healthcare agent may be faced with difficult health care choices, under demanding circumstances. Therefore, it is extremely important that you convey your wishes to your healthcare agent concerning medical decisions and life-sustaining treatments.

Your health care power of attorney has typically the following powers:

- Make medical decisions for you;
- Withdraw medical procedures;
- Retain or discharge medical personnel, physician, nurses and home care;
- Access medical records; and
- Visit you at the hospital and nursing home.

15 Topics to Discuss with Your Health Care Agent

A health care agent is a person you appoint to make medical decisions on your behalf if you are incapacitated or unable to make any decisions. A Living Will (Advanced Directive) expresses your wishes about your health care including, but not limited to, resuscitation, life sustaining treatments (respirator, feeding tube, etc.) and withholding / withdrawing of life sustaining treatments. The Living Will is only effective when you are terminally ill or unconscious and unable to communicate your wishes.

When it comes to making decisions regarding end of life issues, do you know your wishes or have you communicated those wishes to your health care agent? Do you want to be resuscitated should your heart stop? Do you want to be hooked up to a life support system, feeding tube or respirator? What are your feelings about certain medical treatments?

There are no right or wrong or "preferable" answers to these questions. However, you should be able to communicate these answers, based on your own beliefs, wishes and desires, to your health care agent:

1. You're seriously ill and doctors are recommending chemotherapy; would you be willing to endure very severe side effects, such as severe pain, nausea, vomiting or weakness that could last for months, if the chance that you would regain your current health was very low?

2. What do you need for comfort and support as your journey nears death?
3. If you had Alzheimer's disease and it progressed to the point where you could no longer recognize or converse with your love ones; when spoon-feeding was no longer possible, would you want to be fed by a tube into your stomach?
4. If you were terminally ill with a condition that caused much pain, would you want to be sedated, even to the point of unconsciousness, if it were necessary to control your pain?
5. Imagine that you were physically frail and needed help with most routine daily activities such as dressing, bathing, eating, and going to the toilet. You were living in a nursing home although still mentally capable most of the time and became sick with pneumonia for the third time this winter causing hospitalization and pain, would you want aggressive antibiotic treatment again or just comfort care until death?
6. Would you want the following medical treatments?
    - Kidney Dialysis (if kidneys not working)
    - CPR (used if heart stops working)
    - Respirator (unable to breathe)
    - Artificial nutrition (unable to eat food)
    - Artificial hydration (unable to drink fluids)
7. Imagine that you are in a permanent coma and dependent on a feeding tube. Would your medical decisions be guided by any particular religious beliefs or spiritual values?
8. Are some conditions worse than death? If you are housebound, in severe discomfort or pain most of the time, would you want medical treatments to keep you alive?
9. Discuss your current health status and, if any medical problems, how do they affect your ability to function?
10. Do you think that your own doctor should make the final decision about any medical treatments you may require?
11. Would you want to have a hospice team or other palliative care (i.e., comfort care) available to you?
12. Do you have any fears regarding health care and/or death?
13. Do you want to donate parts of your body for transplantation or medical research?

14. What are your thoughts about a memorial or religious service? Where would you like your remains placed? Do you want to be buried or cremated?
15. What else do you feel is important for your agent to know?

A few years ago, I prepared a Medical Power of Attorney and Advance Directive for a client in his early eighties. He chose his son to make medical and end of life decisions for him if he became unable to make these decisions. He was concerned that his spouse or daughter could not make the appropriate choices for him regarding medical treatment and continued life support. Unfortunately, his physician suspects that he now has Dementia. However, my client has peace of mind that his son has the authority to make decisions about his health care needs and his end of life wishes.

I. IRREVOCABLE TRUST

The irrevocable trust is a tool for Medicaid planning and can also be used, in conjunction with life insurance policies, as an estate tax planning strategy. An asset protection trust is commonly termed as an Irrevocable Trust or a Medicaid "Friendly" Trust. The trust is irrevocable. Therefore, the trust cannot be changed or amended after it is established by anyone including the Grantor (owner of the trust). Any property deposited into the trust can only be distributed by the Trustee (manager of the trust), according to the rules and regulations of the trust.

Establishing an Irrevocable Trust

There are certain key provisions that trust-creating documents should contain. The trust instrument should contain an express statement as to its irrevocability. An irrevocable trust is deemed to be unamendable.

The trust should clearly identify all interested parties, including the grantor(s), the trustee(s), and any and all beneficiaries. This is particularly important when a trust has been created because of its federal and estate gift tax or public benefits implications.

To avoid conflicts between beneficiaries, the trust should state the objectives that motivated establishment of the trust. The trust should also specify successor trustees, particularly if a single individual has been designated trustee rather than an institution or business concern, such as a law firm or bank. Any compensation to the trustee should be spelled out, and any processes by which successors are qualified or passed over. If the grantor intends to relieve the trustee of bonding or reporting requirements, the instrument should state such an intention.

The grantor cannot be a beneficiary of the irrevocable trust and it should be expressly stated.

Although Maryland law specifies that trustees have fiduciary powers and obligations, it may be preferable to designate, in writing, the initial and successor trustees' powers. Any limitations on investments contemplated by the grantor should be stated, as well as direction with respect to administering investments such as the right to vote stock, sell assets, and register securities.

The trust instrument should also state that the trustee has the right to remove assets from the state, since such authority may be necessary to serve beneficiaries both currently and in the future, and may also be necessary to seek the most advantageous investments for trust properties. The trustee should also be given powers to combine the property of the trust; to terminate a trust that has become uneconomical; to execute deeds or other documents; to retain agents and other professional services as they become necessary in carrying out the trustee's duties. The right of trustees to resign, and the manner of their resignation, should also be specified.

Funding a Trust

All trust property must be titled in the name of the trust. The comparative complexity or inconvenience of accomplishing this varies according to the nature of the asset being assigned to the trust. Bank accounts, credit union accounts, checking accounts, automobiles, and real property vary considerably in their rules when it comes to changing title. Credit unions often limit granting title in shared accounts to trusts. Customers are often limited to establishing co-title, designating a beneficiary after death, or simply removing funds from the credit union. Certificates of deposit may be treated by some institutions as having been effectively "cashed out" if they are retitled unless specific arrangements are made in advance. This may trigger certain penalties. It is therefore very important to negotiate with an institution before retitling a certificate of deposit.

Checking accounts do not present difficulties as to retitling in the name of a trust. However, checks should be re-titled in the name of the trust. Unless an automobile is extraordinarily expensive and/or a specialty car that appreciates in value, it is generally wise to exclude automobiles from trust planning. This is due to the possibility of transfer taxes, and the potential for frequent changes of ownership or other disposal.

Real property can be assigned to a trust only by deed, which must be recorded at the applicable office of land records. No transfer taxes are imposed unless some form of payment is made, which is usually not the case. Because deeds must be notarized, if a trust is to own real property, the instrument creating the trust must also be notarized.

Taxation of Trusts

Income taxes and transfer (estate and gift) taxes operate by different rules; hence the effects of each on a trust must be analyzed separately. It is advisable to talk with your tax advisor, CPA, etc. regarding the tax ramifications.

Taxpayers who establish revocable trusts do not need to obtain separate Employer Identification Numbers if the grantor or the grantor's spouse serves as trustee. All other trusts must obtain an Employer Identification Number (EIN) with an IRS Form SS-4 and file a tax return on the trust income.

Records and Provision of Copies

Institutions and agents of entities in which a grantor owns interest, stock or assets often request copies of trust documents at the time assets in their firm or institution are conveyed to a trust, but it is often not necessary to provide a copy of the trust if there is a privacy concern.

We have utilized Irrevocable Trusts for many of our clients. We set up the Trust, and add their home, and various other assets into the Trust. After the Trust has been established and funded for five years, the Trust becomes a non countable asset towards paying for the nursing home. We call this part of our pre crisis planning. A client established an Irrevocable Trust in 2008. The client placed their primary residence along with $50,000 into the Trust. In 2015, the client entered a nursing home. We applied and were approved for Medicaid. The assets in the Trust, the primary residence and the $50,000, plus interest, were protected from the nursing home.

J. JOINT TENANCY

Joint Tenancy is where you can own property with another as joint tenants. Joint Tenancy can avoid Probate, because all property held Joint Tenancy carries the "Right of Survivorship." The right of survivorship is where one of the joint tenants dies, his or her ownership share of the joint tenancy property is transferred to and becomes the property of the surviving joint tenant, without the necessity of Probate.

When you die your property will be transferred to the beneficiaries and charities you have named in a Will. This process is called Probate. However, not all property is transferred by your Will. If you title or own property in one of the following, your Will has no effect:

- Joint Tenancy
- Payable on Death
- Named Beneficiaries

Additionally, Joint Tenancy is simpler to establish than a Trust. For example, you open a checking account in both names as Joint Tenants. Therefore both Joint Tenants have complete access to the funds. However, Joint Tenancy does come with risks. If one of the Joint Tenants misappropriates the funds, or they have creditor claims this may cause serious issues for the other Joint Tenants.

It is usually easy to terminate a Joint Tenancy ownership while you and other co-joint tenants are alive.

Another issue with Joint Tenancy is you cannot leave your interest in the Joint Tenancy property to another i.e. in a Will or a Trust. If you name a beneficiary, in a Will or a trust, to inherit your Joint Tenancy share, it will have no consequence, as the proceeds will go directly to the survivor the Joint Tenancy.

In lieu of Joint Tenancy, another form of shared ownership is Tenants in Common. In Tenants In Common there is no "Right of Survivorship" created when you die. Consequently, you can leave your share to a beneficiary, through your Will or trust.

A Tenancy by the Entirety allows married couples to own real property (e.g. a home) as a single legal entity. Consequently, creditors of an individual spouse may not attach and sell the interest of the debtor spouse. Upon the death of one of the spouses, the deceased spouse's interest transfers to the surviving spouse, like the Joint Tenancy, but will not pass through a Will or trust to named beneficiaries.

A number of clients have come to our office, and want to add their children to the title of their home and bank accounts, basically, as joint owners (tenants). I do not recommend this. By adding a joint owner with a right of survivorship to your property (a joint tenant) it will pass 100% of the property to the joint owner upon your death. Consequently, probate is not necessary. However, this can be problematic. For instance, if a child is added to an account, and that child is later sued (e.g. divorce, car accident, etc.), 100% of that account may be subject to the lawsuit, and the parent may be left with no recourse. Also, joint tenancy "overrides" any Last Will and Testament you may have executed. Therefore, if you wish to evenly divide your estate to your children upon your death, and you have assets in joint tenancy, with one of your children, your estate planning goals may not be met. Say, you have three children, and your Estate is worth $300,000. Your desire is to split your Estate evenly, so each child should receive $100,000. However, you have a $50,000 in a checking account, as joint tenancy, with one of your children. Upon your death, the joint tenancy child will receive the $50,000 from the joint checking account and 1/3 of your Estate, $83,333, for a total of

$133,000. As your Estate is worth $300,000 less the $50,000, from the joint checking account, for a total of $250,000. The remaining two children shall receive $83,333 (1/3 of $250,000) each. Thus your goal of equal distribution has not been met.

K. KOREAN WAR VETERANS

The Department of Veteran's Affairs (VA) operates programs for veterans, including, but not limited to:

- Disability compensation;
- Veteran's pensions; and
- Medical care

The Service Connected Disability is a veteran's benefit for those whose disability is connected in any way to their period of service:

- Wounded;
- Injured;
- Ill; and/or
- Aggravated an existing condition

A Non-Service Connected pension is also available to a veteran or a veteran's spouse who require financial help, providing they are a wartime veteran, disabled and over 65. To qualify, the veteran must have at least ninety (90) days active duty and one (1) of these days must be during a war period. The war period consists of:

- World War I – April 6, 1917 through November 11, 1918
- World War II – December 7, 1941 through December 31, 1946
- Korean War – June 27, 1950 through December 31, 1955
- Vietnam War – August 5, 1964 through May 7, 1975
- Persian Gulf War – August 2, 1990 - ongoing.

Additionally, veterans who need help with aid and attendance, at home, assisted living facility, or nursing home may qualify for additional benefits.

Another important benefit to veterans is health care treatment both in patient and out-patient. However the VA has a priority rating for veterans:

- Group 1 – Veterans with service connected disabilities rates 50% or more
- Group 2 – Veterans with service connected disabilities rated 30% - 40%
- Group 3 – Veterans who are former POW, plus service connected disabilities rated 10% - 20%
- Group 4 – Veterans receiving Aid & Attendance
- Group 5 – Veterans with 0% disability with limited income/assets
- Group 6 – All other veterans

The VA has additional programs for veterans like education, vocation, life insurance, home loans, etc. Eligibility requirements vary for each program.

The VA has regional offices and veteran centers throughout the country. For applications, information, and help visit the veterans center. Usually all applications for benefits are processed by the regional offices.

We have helped numerous Veterans obtain Aid and Attendance. I had a Veteran as a client, who was living in an assisted living facility, with a cost of $5,000 per month. I showed the family how to obtain and qualify for Aid and Attendance. The Veteran received approximately $2,000 per month toward the cost of the assisted living facility. The family was thrilled.

L. LONG-TERM CARE INSURANCE

If you can afford the premiums and you are insurable, the best solution to the prospect of significant long-term care costs is long-term care insurance. Most long-term care insurance policies today pay for home care, assisted living and nursing home care. The problem is choosing a good policy and being able to afford it.

Long-term care insurance is a contract between an insurance company and a policy-holder to pay for certain types of coverage under certain conditions. In general, long term care policies are sold by insurance agents to a policy-holder. However, group policies are becoming increasingly available from large employers, membership organizations like AARP, and health maintenance organizations.

Despite the wide range of policy options, there are a few rules of thumb for purchasing a policy. Following these rules tends to drive up the insurance premium, but if an individual is going to invest in long-term care coverage, he or she should buy a good policy.

Buy Enough Coverage for What You Want to Cover

While nursing homes are increasingly expensive, more alternatives to nursing homes exist than ever before. If you cannot afford to purchase sufficient coverage to pay for nursing home care (including anticipated inflation), you may be able to cover the cost of home care or assisted living. In that case you can think of the policy as "avoid nursing home" insurance. It doesn't make much sense to pay insurance premiums and then be bankrupted by nursing home fees because of insufficient coverage. As with other medical expenses, the inflation rate in nursing home fees is quite high.

Buy At Least Five Years of Coverage

After moving to a nursing home, you may want to transfer assets to your children, or to whomever you would like to benefit, if you haven't done so already. Medicaid penalizes such transfers by imposing a period of ineligibility depending on how much you have gifted, if the gift was made during the "look back" period, which is currently five (5) years. After those five years have passed, you can qualify for Medicaid to pay your nursing home costs (provided the assets remaining in your name do not exceed Medicaid's limits.)

Fill Out the Application Completely and Make Sure the Insurance Company Evaluates It Before Issuing the Policy

If, in order to qualify for insurance, you fail to tell the insurer about an illness, the insurance company may refuse you coverage at the time benefits are needed. It is better to be denied a policy and to be able to plan knowing that coverage is not available than to believe that coverage will be forthcoming, only to have it denied when it is needed. Likewise, you should make sure that you purchase from an insurance company that evaluates – or in insurance company parlance "underwrites" – the policy from day one. If not, the company could refuse you coverage when they evaluate the application at a later date.

Compare Insurance Companies and Rates

Make certain that the insurer is rated A or A+ by a service that rates insurance companies. Your coverage will not be very effective if the insurer goes out of business. In addition, rates charged by insurance companies in the long-term care field tend to vary widely. Compare different companies' rates and offerings before making your decision.

Which Spouse Gets the Coverage?

Often, a married couple will be able to afford coverage for only one spouse. Looking at statistics alone, the wife should purchase the policy. In our society women tend to live longer than men. The result is that women are much more likely than men to end up in a nursing home for a long period of time. In addition, the Medicaid rules provide some protection for the spouse of a nursing home resident. For these reasons, the best bet for couples who can afford the premiums for one policy only is to purchase it for the wife. Couples should bear in mind, however, that this is playing the odds and is not a sure thing.

Can You Afford Long-Term Care Insurance?

A rule of thumb is that payment of the long-term care insurance premium should not affect your standard of living. Thus, premiums are affordable if they are paid with money that you would otherwise set aside to add to savings. An alternative would be to purchase an annuity that pays sufficient benefits to cover the long-term care insurance premiums.

The Tax Deductibility of Long-Term Care Insurance Premiums

Under the Health Insurance Portability and Accountability Act, also known as "Kennedy-Kassebaum," passed in 1996, "qualified" long-term care insurance policies receive special tax treatment. To be "qualified," policies issued on or after January 1, 1997, must adhere to regulations established by the National Association of Insurance Commissioners adopted in January 1993. Among the requirements are that the policy must offer the consumer the options of "inflation" and "nonforfeiture" protection, although the consumer can choose not to purchase these features.

The policies must also offer both activities of daily living (ADL) and cognitive impairment triggers. "Triggers" are conditions that must be present for a policy to be activated. Under the ADL trigger, benefits may begin only when the beneficiary needs assistance with at least two of six ADL's. The ADL's are: eating, toileting, transferring, bathing, dressing, or continence. In addition, a licensed health care practitioner must certify that the need for assistance with the ADL's is reasonably expected to continue for at least 90 days. Under a cognitive impairment trigger, coverage begins when the individual has been certified to require substantial supervision to protect him or her from threats to health and safety due to cognitive impairment.

Policies purchased before January 1, 1997, will be grandfathered and treated as "qualified" as long as they have been approved by the insurance commissioner of the state in which they are sold. Most individual policies must receive approval from the insurance commission in the state they are sold, while most group policies do not require this approval. To determine whether a particular policy will be grandfathered, policyholders should check with their insurance broker or with their state's insurance agency. Premiums for "qualified" long-term care policies may be tax deductable, check with your tax advisor/CPA.

Consult With a Qualified Agent

If you are considering long-term care insurance, you need to consult with a qualified professional to determine whether you can afford this type of coverage and whether the policy you are considering meets necessary standards.

Long-term care insurance has attracted much media attention, and many insurance agents are now selling it. However, long-term care insurance is a complex product that should be approached with caution.

One factor to consider is whether the agent has a professional designation in providing advice about long-term care. However, recommendations from friends and other advisors are also very important because they will have personal knowledge of the experience and integrity of the people they recommend.

Also, if you can afford to purchase long term care insurance I recommend that you do. The economic and political climate now and in the future is uncertain. Will Medicare or Medicaid be available in the future, nobody knows? So you are better to take care of yourself rather than relying on politicians and the government.

M. MEDICARE & MEDICAID

MEDICARE

Medicare is a federal program that helps seniors and the disabled pay some of their medical costs:

- Part A – basically, hospital insurance
- Part B – medical insurance
- Part C – Medicare Advantage Plans
- Part D – prescription drugs

Part A – Hospital Insurance

Most people, age 65 and older are automatically eligible for Medicare Part A, if they qualify for Social Security Retirement benefits or civil service retirement benefits. However, if you do not automatically qualify, you can enroll in the Medicare Hospital Insurance program for a fee. If you qualify for Medicare Part A, you do not pay any premiums, it is free.

For coverage under Part A - Hospital Insurance, the care and treatment must be medically and reasonably necessary i.e. care can only be provided at a hospital or nursing home. Medicare Part A will not pay if you receive treatment as a hospital outpatient, doctor's office or at your home.

Medicare Part A pays only a certain amount of the hospital bill. You must pay the hospital insurance deductible. For the first 60 days of a hospital stay, Medicare Part A will pay all the cost of covered essential services. Medicare Part A will not pay for televisions or telephones i.e. non-essential services. After 61 days, and through the 90th day, you will pay a "co-insurance amount".

Additionally, Medicare Part A will pay during the benefit period. A benefit period consists of the time you are hospitalized. The period begins when you are "admitted" to the hospital and continues until you have been out of the hospital for 60 continuous days. If you are discharged, then re-admitted, discharged and then re-admitted, but within 60 days, these days will be part of the same benefit period.

Part B – Medical Insurance

To be eligible for Medicare Part B you must be 65 or older and either a U.S. citizen or a lawful resident of the U.S. for at least 5 years. Also, you must enroll in Medicare Part B, and everyone pays a monthly premium. Medicare Part B pays for basic medical expenses, for example:

- Doctors;
- Clinics and Laboratories;
- Ambulance – if medically necessary;
- Medical Supplies; and
- Preventive Screening Exams.

However, not all services are covered. Therefore, you must be cognizant of the benefits available to you.

Medicare does not cover all major medical expenses like glasses, hearing aids, dentures and other medical services. Also, Medicare Part B usually only covers about 80% of the medical service cost. Therefore, you are responsible for the remaining 20% (see Medigap Insurance). Additionally, you must pay a deductible of your covered medical services for the year.

Part C – Medicare Advantage Plans

Medicare Advantage Plans are managed care plans, e.g. your care is managed by an insurance company. Consequently, you receive care from specific doctors, clinics, and hospitals – the insurance companies' network. The managed care is usually in two forms:

(1) HMO – Health Maintenance Organization
(2) Fee for Service

HMO

The HMO is the most restrictive Medicare Advantage Plan. However, it is the least expensive. The HMO maintains a "network" of doctors and other health care providers. Consequently, you must receive care and treatment from a "network" provider. If you use a non-network provider, the HMO will not cover this cost, thus you will be responsible for the cost.

As a HMO, member, you select a primary care doctor from the network. Therefore, for all medical issues you must see this doctor first, i.e. gatekeeper, and the doctor will make a referral, if you need to see a specialist.

FEE FOR SERVICE

The Fee for Service offers the members greater freedom in the choice of their doctors and medical providers. Unlike the HMO, the fee for service does not have a "network" of medical providers but you may utilize any healthcare provider that accepts Medicare patients.

However, your out of pocket expenses are higher with an "out of network" provider than the "in network" provider.

To evaluate a Medicare Advantage Plan, you must review its coverage and costs. A summary of benefits usually identifies the plan coverage.

Part D – Prescription Drugs

As of January 1, 2006, Medicare began covering some prescription drug costs, under Medicare Part D. Medicare Part D is provided by private insurance companies i.e. Blue Cross/Blue Shield, AETNA etc. that offer Medicare approved Prescription Drug Plans ("PDP").

To be eligible for Medicare Part D, you must be enrolled in Medicare Part A or B.

For coverage, you must enroll. The cost of coverage is very complicated, as each insurance company has a different cost for their plan coverage. Also, deductibles may be charged, and they also vary from each insurance company and their coverage plans.

Additionally, your deductibles may even vary for each prescription.

Also, as part of Medicare Part D, there is a gap of coverage (called The Doughnut Hole). This also can vary for each coverage plan. When you have paid a certain amount of deductible, your plan may pay nothing until you reach the "catastrophic" amount, then the plan will begin to pay again.

Under Medicare Part D each insurance company has a plan that includes a formulary i.e. what drugs the plan covers or does not. Under the plan, if a drug is not covered under the formulary, the plan may not pay any portion of the cost; nor will this cost count toward your Part D deductible or the coverage gap.

Medigap insurance

If you have Medicare Part A and B, a serious illness can cause financial ruin. In fact, the most common cause of Bankruptcy for seniors is unpaid medical bills.

Medicare does not cover all medical costs. Therefore, to protect yourself you should purchase insurance, known as "Medigap" polices.

As stated, Medicare Part A pays for hospital coverage. However, you must pay a deductible or the hospital daily coinsurance over 60 days. Also, Medicare Part B has major gaps as well. One of the biggest gaps is going in a nursing home for rehabilitation. If you are admitted into a hospital for more than three overnights and are transferred to a nursing home, your rehabilitative stay is covered 100% for the first twenty days. From twenty one days to a hundred days you are going to have to pay a co-pay. This is coming out of your pocket unless you have a Medigap policy. If you have a Medigap policy, the Medigap policy will pick up the co-pay. This gap can be a major issue for seniors. At this moment in time the hospital may not "admit" you, but you are under "observation." If you are under observation then transferred to a nursing home, Medicare will not pay for the nursing home stay. So, if you are in the nursing home for two months, your cost will be approximately twenty thousand dollars (2 months of nursing home stay times $10,000 per month). Note if Medicare does not cover a medical treatment, neither will the Medigap policy.

Review the coverage of the Medigap policy, as policies vary, and also review potential premium issues - age, no age rating, attained age and pre-existing condition coverage. Obviously, the larger the policy coverage the higher the cost of the policy.

You must determine not only if a Medigap policy is right for you, but which insurance company offers the best policy and the best price.

MEDICAID

Difference Between Medicare and Medicaid

Most people are confused between Medicare and Medicaid. Basically, Medicare deals with medical costs, doctors, hospitals and prescription drugs. Medicare is available to you, if you are 65 or older, regardless of your income and assets. However, Medicaid pays for long term care-nursing home costs, and you must qualify for this government program by having a low income and limited assets.

Introduction

Medicaid is a Federal and State program. The Federal government provides guidelines. The State is permitted to make their own rules providing they stay within the Federal guidelines. To qualify for Medicaid you usually, require to be in a nursing home, require skilled care, have limited income and assets.

If you qualify for Medicaid, then your costs of care, room and board, pharmacy and incidentals will be paid for.

Eligibility

Medicaid is available to individuals who meet certain eligibility conditions:

- Need skilled care (usually in a nursing home)
- Limited assets
- Limited income

Skilled Care

To meet the skilled care requirement the nursing home will perform a medical assessment. Establishing medical eligibility is usually not a problem.

Limited Assets

The main challenge is verifying limited income and assets. If you are a single person, in Maryland, the only assets that you can maintain are less than $2,500; life insurance up to $1,500; a burial plot; and prepay your funeral. Every other asset is considered an available asset to pay the nursing home.

If you are married, some savings, your primary residence, a car, burial plots and a prepaid funeral are non-countable assets. Therefore, savings account, checking accounts, stocks, bonds, mutual funds, 401k, IRA, in excess of the non-countable asset allowances, second homes, and other cars are considered countable assets. Therefore, these assets in excess of the resource limitations are available assets. Thus, you will not qualify for Medicaid, until these available assets have been "spent down."

In lieu of "spending down" assets on the nursing home, you can "spend down" assets with proper asset protection planning techniques.

Generally, the purpose of an asset protection plan is to make the person eligible for Medicaid, without spending all of their assets on the nursing home i.e. preserving as much of your resources for you or your loved one.

Asset protection planning occurs in two stages:

- Preplanning
- Crisis

PREPLANNING

The preplanning stage occurs when you are expected to enter a nursing home sometime in the future. Generally, preplanning techniques include long term care insurance, gifting and utilizing irrevocable trusts.

CRISIS

Crisis planning occurs when you enter the nursing home without any preplanning and you are not expected to return home or to the assisted living facility. Consequently, you will be paying the nursing home with your hard earned savings. This type of planning is more common, as most seniors believe they will not require a nursing home stay. However, when the nursing home stay is a reality, you need to address it.

Why Seek Asset Protection Advice?

As life expectances and nursing home costs increase, the challenge quickly becomes; how to pay for the cost of care. Many people cannot afford to pay the $10,000 plus per month to the nursing home and those who can may find their life savings wiped out in a matter of months.

Limited Income

If you are a single person, and your income is less than the nursing home monthly cost, you will qualify for Medicaid, providing you meet the other eligibility criteria.

For most people, their monthly income does not exceed the monthly nursing home cost i.e. $10,000 plus per month. For the spouse, residing at home (the "community spouse") they are allowed to keep a minimum monthly income, ranging from $1,991.25 to $2,980 in 2016. If the Community Spouse does not have at least $1,991.25 in income, then he or she is allowed to receive income from the nursing home spouse in an amount to reach the $1,991.25 amount. The nursing home spouse's remaining income goes to the nursing home.

Disqualification

Certain gifts or transfers for less than fair market value will make the Medicaid applicant temporarily ineligible for Medicaid, depending on the amount of the gift or transfer. Gifts or transfers in Maryland, within the look back period of 5 years, will cause one month of ineligibility for every $7,940 (as of 2016) gifted away. The penalty period begins to run when the applicant is otherwise eligible for Medicaid, but for the gift. In short, gifting, of any kind, to your children or other family members, religious organizations or charities can cause major problems with Medicaid eligibility.

Estate Recovery

Following the death of a Medicaid recipient the State shall recover from his or her Estate whatever benefits the State paid for the Medicaid recipient's care. For example, if the Medicaid recipient owned a $100,000 home and State expended $200,000 on the recipient's care, the State would be entitled to receive the $100,000 from the sale of the home.

Some Mistakes

We have heard the following mistakes of Medicaid and Estate Planning:

- Listening to the layman myths of Medicaid Planning, which are usually erroneous and could cost your family its home and assets.
- Believing that a Will will avoid probate. In fact, a Will requires probate and the delays and expense that go with it.
- Naming one child as a co-owner of real estate or bank accounts, and believing that the Will (which requires equal distribution between all children) controls the distribution. The Senior's co-owner or beneficiary on the account or deed controls.
- Failure to use a Quitclaim Deed in the proper circumstance – such Deed is inexpensive and if done correctly could avoid Medicaid claims and Probate administration.
- Failure to have Powers of Attorney in place as part of your Estate Plan. The financial and/or medical Power of Attorney will assist you in Medicaid Planning.
- Using form Wills bought at a store, without consulting an Elder Law lawyer. Trouble abounds in these documents. It is penny-wise and pound-foolish.
- Failure to obtain a Revocable Living Trust (RLT), in order to avoid probate and manage your affairs if you become incapacitated. Husband and wife can protect each other, and provide for children.

- Failure to use Trusts, in order to avoid excessive Federal and State Taxation of their estates and nursing home costs.
- Failure to use the tools of Medicaid Planning while you are in a pre-crisis stage.

Medicaid Planning for Married People

Don and Barb were high school sweethearts who lived in Frederick, Maryland, their entire adult lives. Two weeks ago, Don and Barb celebrated their 51st anniversary. Yesterday, Barb, who has Alzheimer's, wandered away from home. Hours later she was found sitting on a street curb, talking incoherently. She was taken to a hospital and treated for dehydration. Don came to see me after their family doctor discusses with him placing Barb in a nursing home. He tells you they both grew up during the Depression and have always tried to save something every month. Their assets, totaling $100,000, not including their house, are as follows:

```
Savings account ......................................... $15,000
CDs ............................................................ $45,000
Money Market account ............................... $37,000
Checking account ....................................... $3,000
Residence (no mortgage) ........................... $80,000
```

Don gets social security and pension checks totaling $1,500 each month. Barb's check is $450. His eyes fill with tears as he says, "At $10,000 to the nursing home every month, our entire life savings will be gone in less than one year!" What's more, Don is concerned that he won't be able to pay Barb's monthly nursing home bill because a neighbor told him that nursing home will be entitled to all of their social security checks.

However, there is some good news for Don and Barb. It's possible he will get to keep his income and their assets... and still have the state Medicaid program pay Barb's nursing home costs. While the process may take a little while, the end result will be worth it.

To apply for Medicaid, he will have to go through the Frederick County (County – where they reside) Department of Social Services (DSS). If he does things strictly according to the way DSS tells him, he will only be able to keep about 1/2 of their assets (or about $50,000) plus he will keep his income. But the results can actually be much better than the traditional spend-down, which everyone talks about. Don might be able to turn the spend down amount of roughly $50,000 into an income stream for him that will increase his income and meet the Medicaid spend down virtually right away.

In other words, if handled properly Barb may be eligible for Medicaid from the first month that she goes into the nursing home. Please note this will not work in every case. That's why it is important to have an Elder Law attorney guide you through the system and the Medicaid process to find the strategies that will be most beneficial in your situation. So, he will have to get advice from someone who knows how to navigate the system. But with proper advice he may be able to keep most of what he and Barb have worked so hard for. This is possible because the law does not intend to impoverish one spouse because the other needs care in a nursing home. This is certainly an example where knowledge of the rules and how to apply them can be used to resolve Don and Barb's dilemma. Of course, proper Medicaid planning differs according to the relevant facts and circumstances of each situation.

N. NURSING HOME

A nursing home is a facility for chronically ill residents who need twenty-four hour care either skilled care and/or help with at least two activities of daily living. Consequently, admission to a nursing home is based upon medical need, and a doctor's evaluation is required.

Each resident is required to have an individualized care plan. Subsequently, the care plan is reviewed, and updated every three months. The care plan is prepared by nursing home staff including resident physician with input from the resident or resident's advocate (power of attorney).

Most nursing homes remind you of a hospital setting. Usually, residents are in a semi-private room. Therefore, it is very important to the resident's contentment that the roommate be compatible i.e. common interests, language, habits, etc.

In 1987 congress passed the Nursing Home Reform Act. Therefore, nursing homes are regulated by the Federal and State governments. Consequently, each nursing home must have an administrator and director of nursing. Also, nursing homes must provide services and activities to attain or maintain the highest practicable physical, mental, and psycho-social well-being of each resident in accordance with a written plan of care. Generally, a nursing home facility must have a licensed nurse on duty, twenty four hours a day.

As part of nursing home supervision, the state conducts inspections of the facility, staff and residents.

The ABC's of Elder Law & Estate Planning

Under the Nursing Home Reform Act:

- A nursing home resident can:
  - Choose his or her own physician;
  - Obtain information regarding treatment;
  - Participate in care; and
  - Accept or refuse treatment.

- A nursing home must:
  - Provide polices/manuals to the resident, or make them available;
  - Provide reasonable accommodation;
  - Not require third party guarantee of payments as a condition of admission; and
  - Not restrain physically or chemically the resident.

State Law generally limits reasons for involuntary transfer or discharge from the nursing home. The nursing home must provide written notice at least thirty days in advance of the proposed discharge/transfer that includes:

- Reason for the action;
- Appeal rights;
- Availability of mediation.

If the resident requests an appeal he or she provides a written request to the Office of Administrative Hearings.

Long Term Nursing Home costs are paid by:

- Private pay;
- Long Term Care Insurance; and
- Medicaid.

Rehabilitation Nursing Home costs are usually paid by

- Medicare;
- Private Pay;

David Wingate

- Health Insurance; and/or
- Long Term Care Insurance.

All nursing home facilities have a contract between the facility and the resident. Within this contract, are all the terms and conditions regarding the facility and the resident's care. It is important to consult with an elder law attorney before you sign this contract.

How are you going to pay for the nursing home? Medicare will only pay for a limited amount of rehabilitative nursing home care and Medicaid only pays for long term nursing home care, if and when, you qualify for Medicaid. Unfortunately, most people pay privately at over $10,000 per month. Thus it does not take long for their hard earning savings to be wiped out by the nursing home. I cannot tell you how many spouses or family members come to our office and state they need to apply for Medicaid, after being or their loved one has been in the nursing home for a number of years. After, this time period their savings have been decimated. That's why we are here to help people like you avoid having your savings wiped out by the nursing home. I had a client whose mother was in a nursing home. The cost of her care was $10,500 per month. I showed the family how to protect $100,000, and how to qualify for Medicaid. They were overjoyed.

O. OMBUDSMAN

HAVE YOU HEARD THESE NURSING HOME PROBLEMS?

- "Medicaid does not pay for the service that you want."
- "The nursing staff will determine the care that you receive."
- "We don't have enough staff to accommodate individual schedules."
- "We don't have enough staff. You should hire you own private-duty aide."
- "If we don't tie your father into his chair he may fall or wander away from the nursing home. There's just no way we can always be watching him."
- "Your mother needs medication in order to make her more manageable."
- "We must insert a feeding tube into your father because he is taking too long to eat."
- Your children can visit you only during visiting hours."
- "We can't admit your mother unless you sign the admission Contract as a "Responsible Party."
- "Please sign this arbitration agreement. It's no big deal."
- "Medicare can't pay for your nursing home care because we have determined that you need custodial care only."
- "We must discontinue therapy services because you aren't making progress."
- "We can't give you therapy services because your Medicare reimbursement has expired, and Medicaid doesn't pay for therapy."

- "Because you are no longer eligible for Medicare reimbursement, you must leave this Medicare-certified bed."
- "Even though you're now financially eligible for Medicaid payment, we don't have an available Medicaid bed for you."
- "We don't have to readmit you from the hospital because your bed-hold period has expired."
- "You must pay any amount set by the nursing home for extra charges."
- "We have no available space in which residents or family members could meet."
- You must leave the nursing home because you are a difficult resident."
- You must leave the nursing home because you are refusing medical treatment."

You or your advocate (power of attorney) should demand that the nursing home comply with the Nursing Home Reform Law. Your first step is to communicate your complaints with the nursing home's representative. If you are not receiving satisfactory answers from the nursing home, then utilize the services of the Ombudsman. The Ombudsman provides assistance to residents of nursing home facilities:

- Identify, investigate and resolve complaints;
- Provide services to protect residents' safety, welfare and rights; and
- Inform residents about available services;

Under Federal Law Ombudsman have access to nursing homes and their residents. Consequently, the Ombudsman is valuable assistant in a dispute with the nursing home.

Unfortunately, the Ombudsman has limited powers. Unlike the state inspectors the Ombudsman cannot impose any penalties against the nursing home.

If, after individual advocacy and the Ombudsman intervention, the nursing home refuses to amend its position, you have basically two options:

- Contract the supervising government agency; or
- Hire an attorney to pursue the nursing home.

P. PROBATE

Whether your spouse has just passed away or you've lost your mom or dad, the emotional trauma of losing a loved one often comes with a bewildering array of financial and legal issues demanding attention. Take your time – while bills need to be paid, they can wait a week or two without any real repercussions. It's more important that you and your family have time to grieve. Financial matters can wait.

When you are ready, meet with an attorney to review the steps necessary to probate the Will. Probate is a legal process that includes:

- Filing the Will and petitioning the probate court to appoint the personal representative.
- Collect the assets. This means that you need to find out about everything the deceased owned and file a list or inventory with the court.
- Pay the bills and taxes. If an estate tax return is due, it must be filed within nine months of the date of death.
- Distribute property to the heirs. Generally, personal representatives do not pay out all of the estate assets until the period for creditors to make claims runs out – 6 months. The average length for Probate is about one year.
- Finally, you must file an account with the court listing any income to the estate since the date of death and all expenses and estate distributions. Therefore, the actual probate functions are mostly administrative.

The Personal Representative (Executor), who will be appointed by the deceased person in their Will, has the responsibility to manage the estate, and ensure that the deceased person's affairs are carried out.

The Personal Representative is entitled to a fee for their services.

Usually, the typical probate process takes about one year. Consequently, to avoid this costly and time-consuming process you can:

- Prepare a trust;
- Manage your finances by designating;
  - Beneficiary;
  - Payable on Debts;
  - Joint Tenancy;
- Gifting before you die;
- Designate Beneficiary for:
  - IRA's
  - 401K;
  - Life Insurance.

To avoid Probate we recommend a Revocable Trust over Joint Tenancy. A revocable living trust ("trust") is an effective approach to transfer property at your death and thus avoid probate. Basically, a trust is an estate planning document which allows an individual to direct another person (the trustee) to manage property during the individual's life and to distribute property upon the individual's death, according to the individual's specific wishes. Unlike a Will, a trust is not probated. However, similar to a Will, a trust may not avoid Maryland estate and inheritance tax.

Proper estate planning is a must if you want to be sure your property will pass upon your death to your loved ones according to your wishes.

For instance, if you have young children, it is crucial for you to have a Will and a trust in place because minor children cannot take title to property in their own names. Additionally, it is important to arrange for the care of your minor children after your death, and it is critical to be sure that, where possible, the person who will be caring for your children will have access to the funds to properly care for them.

In addition, some people are not emotionally equipped to handle sums of money they receive outright, and it is common to see individuals who have received an inheritance to quickly spend that inheritance in the matter of a few short weeks or months. Proper, thoughtful estate planning can avoid this and insure that everyone is protected and your life's savings, no matter how large or small, are not squandered.

Before taking any action to avoid probate or establish a trust, you should consult an attorney who can examine your specific situation and advise you accordingly.

Q. QUALIFICATION FOR MEDICAID

To qualify for Medicaid (Medical Assistance) you must have limited assets and income. Regrettably, most nursing home residents spend all their savings on the nursing home and then file for Medicaid. However, there are legal ways to protect your assets from the nursing home.

For a married couple a number of assets are non-countable in determining eligibility:

- A car;
- Furniture and household goods;
- Your home, providing your spouse resides in it, and depending on its value;
- Life insurance policy up to $1,500;
- Burial plots;
- Prepaid funeral; and
- Community Spouse Resource Amount, equal to one-half of the married couple nonexempt assets in amount between $23,844 and $119,220, as of 2016.

Therefore, to qualify for Medicaid, the institutional spouse (spouse in the nursing home) must have assets below $2,500 in Maryland. Note that Medicaid rules vary from state to state.

For a single person, a number of assets are non-countable to determine eligibility:

- Personal effects in the nursing home room;
- Life insurance up to $1,500;
- Burial plot;
- Prepaid funeral;
- Below $2,500

For most people, they usually have too many assets to qualify for Medicaid. Consequently, if your assets exceed the above you are in a "spend down" before you qualify for Medicaid. However, there are lawful ways to transfer these assets so that you can qualify for Medicaid without spending all your assets on the nursing home. Medicaid Planning for Married People see M. Medicare & Medicaid.

One way is to transfer assets that make you eligible for Medicaid into an Irrevocable Trust, five years before you enter the nursing home. Consequently, those transferred assets will be protected from the nursing home.

Also, if married, you can transfer assets into a non-countable asset i.e. prepaid funeral or your home. For the home:

- Pay off the mortgage;
- Perform home improvements; and/or
- Purchase a home or new home.

Another way to protect your assets, if married, is to purchase a "Medicaid" annuity, see A. Annuity. You pay a sum of money to an insurance company to purchase an annuity. If the annuity meets all the Medicaid specifications, the sum of money is no longer considered part of the married couple eligibility assets; even it purchase within the five year look back period. The annuity will pay a specified monthly amount to the community spouse, for a set period of time.

Medicaid Planning for Single People

Frances was a good daughter. For as long as she could remember, she'd been in the role of caregiver.

When she was little, and Mom was hospitalized for three and a half weeks, Frances had taken over running the family...even though she was only 13. And that wasn't the only time.

It seemed like Frances had finally escaped that role, until three years ago when Mom had a stroke. Since Mom could no longer care for herself, Frances moved back home and took over Mom's care. And she's been doing it for the past three years, but now it's gotten to the point where Mom needs more care than Frances can give.

Mom owns a $150,000 house and she would like to give the house to Frances as a way of saying thank you for all that Frances has done for her. But when Mom and Frances checked around, they're told that if they gift the house to Frances, Mom will be ineligible for Medicaid for a number years and it may even be a criminal act!

They come to me in tears. I calmly told them that there's a provision in the Federal Law (42 U.S.C. § 1396P (c)(2)(a) which is binding in Maryland. The law states that you can give a home to an adult child who resided in the home for at least two years, if the child provided care which permitted Mom to stay at home rather than in an institution or facility.

In other words, if a child moves back home and cares for a parent, and if that child's care has kept the parent out of a nursing home for at least the last two years, then the home may be given to the child without Medicaid penalties.

So how should Frances document her care for Mom? The best thing would be to keep a log or journal that sets forth specific incidents or events that, but for the child's care, might have resulted in Mom's institutionalization. For instance, note things like gas burners not being shut off, water left running in the tub, Mom's wandering or other medically dangerous actions.

In addition, it would be helpful to have statements from other family members or neighbors telling of any events or circumstances that reinforce Frances's position. Finally, it would be most helpful to have a letter from a physician and/or visiting nurse or home health care provider saying that Frances's care did in fact keep Mom out of the nursing home for at least two years.

I explained this to Frances and her Mom and they are both delighted that all of Frances's good deeds will not go unrewarded. The house may be given to Frances and Mom can still qualify for Medicaid.

FYI: There are other situations where the home may be transferred without penalty. They include transfers to the following:

- the spouse;
- a minor, blind or disabled child;
- a sibling who has an equity interest in the home and who has resided there for at least one year before the Medicaid applicant became institutionalized.

R. REVOCABLE LIVING TRUST

A revocable living trust ("trust") is an effective approach to transfer property at your death and avoiding probate. Basically, a trust is a legal document that transfers property, that you have placed in the trust, to named beneficiaries, i.e. a Will substitute to avoid probate. The person who establishes the terms and provisions of the trust is called the Grantor. As the Grantor you can revoke and/or revise the trust at any time prior to your death. The Trustee is basically, the manager of the trust. The people or group who acquire the trust property, after your death, are the beneficiaries.

Three major decisions in creating a trust are:

- What property to include in the trust;
- Who is the successor trustee, if you are the trustee? and
- Who is the beneficiary?

You can place most if not all of your property and real property into the trust e.g. your home, checking and savings accounts, stocks, bonds, businesses, etc.

Who will be the successor trustee to you if you become incapacitated or die? The successor trustee is the manager of the trust after you. Also, they will distribute the trust property to the beneficiaries after your death. Your successor trustee should be someone that you trust to perform this duty, and willing to do it. Generally, most Grantors will choose their spouse or children as successor trustees. However, sometimes if your child has little or no financial management skills, issues with drugs or alcohol, it may be appropriate to choose another successor trustee.

Beneficiaries are the people or groups you designate to receive your trust property of after your death. Ordinarily, each spouse names the other as their beneficiary. Also, you can leave different percentages to your children, person or group. To add property to the trust you can set up accounts within the trust i.e. checking, savings and transfer title to the trust i.e. home.

As Grantor, you can amend the trust by preparing an amendment to the trust, sign it and have it notarized. Also, you can revoke the trust by a signed and notarized document.

Whenever a "major life event" occurs, I always recommend that you review your Will and trusts. Your current legal documents may no longer be appropriate. You may want to make changes that reflect your new circumstances. Being diagnosed with an illness such as Alzheimer's disease is a "major life event" worthy of review. The plans that were put into place when you were healthy may no longer be appropriate.

For instance, many clients set up what are referred to as "sweetheart Wills" in which each spouse leaves everything to the other spouse, and then at the death of the second spouse, to their children. This may be the wrong way to set things up now, given one spouse's illness. It may be that things can be arranged in a better fashion so that if the "healthy spouse" passes away first, the assets can be put into a trust to benefit the spouse who is suffering from dementia or be passed down to the children to protect those assets from Medicaid. This is where specific legal planning with an attorney experienced in dealing with dementia patients is critical.

S. SUPPLEMENTAL (SPECIAL) NEEDS TRUST

If your child or grandchild has special needs, and receiving government benefits, and they inherit assets in excess of two thousand dollars, they could lose their government benefits. However, by creating a Supplemental (Special) Needs Trust, the parent or grandparent can support the child with disabilities without the possibility of the child or grandchild losing their government benefits. Basically, the child with disabilities has no control over the trust assets, but is the beneficiary of the trust assets. The trustee of the Supplemental (Special) Needs Trust can utilize the principal and/or income for the child's benefits providing those needs are not covered by government benefits. However, the special needs child cannot be the trustee i.e. manager of the trust.

Grandparents: The Dos and Don'ts of Planning for Your Grandchild(ren) with Special Needs.

I have found that most grandparents want the best for their children and grandchildren. They often give gifts while alive, or make provisions for their loved ones after they are deceased. Grandparents who are in a position to leave money to grandchildren often want to do something for their grandchild(ren) with special needs. They often worry about a severely handicapped or disabled grandchild, who may need additional assets or assistance to lead a quality life. Grandparents are sometimes told not to leave their grandchild(ren) with special needs anything because the child(ren) may lose government benefits. People are often confused as to what to do or not to do.

Grandparents can leave money to their grandchild(ren) with special needs.

There are very special ways to do it!

- Money has to be left in such a way so that government benefits are not lost. Assets in excess of $2,000 will cause the loss of certain government benefits for the person with special needs.
- Money should not be left to the grandchild directly, but should be left to a special needs trust.
- The special needs trust was developed to manage resources while maintaining the individual's eligibility for government benefits. The trust is maintained by a trustee on behalf of the person with special needs. The trustee has discretion to manage the money in the trust and decides how the money is used. The money must be used for supplemental purposes only. It should only supplement, or add to benefits (food, shelter or clothing) that the government already provides through Supplementary Security Income (SSI). It must not supplant or replace government benefits. If properly structured by a knowledgeable special needs attorney, the special needs trust assets will not count towards the $2,000 SSI or SSDI limits for an individual.

Brief Summary of Do's and Don'ts!

Do's:

- Make provisions for your grandchild(ren) with special needs. Leave money to the child's special needs trust.
    - The special needs trust is the only way to leave money without losing government benefits.

- Coordinate all planning with the child's parents or other relatives.
  - Notify the parents when you plan for grandchild(ren). Plan with others.

- Leave life insurance, survivorship whole life policies and annuities to the child's special needs trust.
  - The special needs trust can be named as the policy beneficiary. When the insured or annuitant dies, the death benefit is paid to the special needs trust. The special needs trust then has a lump sum of money to be used in caring for the grandchild(ren) with special needs.

- Consult with trained financial and legal professionals with specialties in special needs estate planning.

Don'ts:

- Do not disinherit your grandchild(ren) with special needs.
  - Money can be now left to a properly drawn up special needs trust. It does not make sense to disinherit any of your grandchild(ren) with special needs.

- Don't give money to your grandchild(ren) with special needs under UGMA or UTMA (Uniform Gift or Transfer To Minors Act).
  - Money automatically belongs to the child(ren) upon reaching legal age. Government benefits can be lost!

- Don't leave money directly to a grandchild with special needs through a will.
  - Money left will be a countable asset of the child and may cause the loss of government benefits.

- Don't leave money to a poorly set up trust.
  - Money left in an improperly drafted trust can result in the loss of government benefits.

- Do not leave money to relatives to "keep or hold" for the child with special needs.
  - The money can be attached to a lawsuit, divorce, liability claim or other judgment against the relative.

T. TRANSFERRING ASSETS TO QUALIFY FOR MEDICAID

As you plan to make gifts in your elder years, you need to know about federal estate and gift taxes, income taxes, Medicaid law, real estate law, estate law, and wills and trusts. Your first step should be to consult an attorney.

The Internal Revenue Service defines a gift as "any voluntary transfer of property from a donor (you) to a donee (another) without what is called full and adequate consideration (basically, money)." A gift occurs when the donor gives up control over the transferred asset. Your gift to anyone during a calendar year will be a "reportable gift" if it exceeds the annual exemption amount (presently $14,000 in 2016). Your payment of educational or medical expenses for another individual is not generally subject to federal gift tax.

The value of a gift for federal gift tax purposes is the "fair market value" of the property transferred. Fair market value is generally defined as the "price which would probably be agreed upon by a seller willing to sell and a buyer willing to buy where both have knowledge of the facts." A gift tax return should be filed in April when you file your personal income tax return if taxable gifts have occurred, or if a married couple desires to "split" a gift.

Under the Deficit Reduction Act of 2005, gifts made after February 8, 2006 can make you ineligible for Medicaid long-term care benefits many years after the gift is made. Medicaid caseworkers will be looking for gifts going back five years. It is therefore very risky for seniors to make gifts of any size if they might need nursing home care within that window of time. Only those with sufficient resources to pay privately for nursing home care for five years can ignore the new Medicaid transfer penalties. Nursing home care can cost over $10,000 per month in Maryland, so seniors must proceed cautiously before making any gifts.

If you transfer assets for no consideration or for less than fair market value, this is a gift. If you apply for Medicaid soon after marking a gift, you will be subject to a period of ineligibility for Medicaid benefits. When you have submitted your Medicaid application the caseworker will examine all of your bank records, 401K, IRA's etc. to determine if you made any gifts with in the "five year look back" period. The "look back" period for outright gifts and disposals of assets, in Maryland, is five years from the point when you are eligible for receiving the Medicaid benefits. If you need Medicaid benefits, and you have gifted some assets away, the penalty period is determined by dividing the amount of the gift by the average cost of a nursing home in Maryland, currently $7,940 (in 2016). Therefore, if you are eligible for Medicaid, but gifted your family member, say $79,400 one year ago, this would create a penalty period of ten months. (Gift $79,400 divided by nursing home divisor $7,940 = 10 months). Consequently, you would be ineligible for Medicaid for ten months, and you would have to pay the nursing home privately for ten months. Thus, if you make a transfer, within the five year look back period, you should beware of the consequences.

While most transfers within the 5 year look back period of Medicaid will cause a period of ineligibility, certain transfers are exempt. You may transfer the following assets, without any penalty, to:

- Your spouse;
- Your child, if blind or permanently disabled; and
- A special needs trust, for the sole benefit of a disabled person, under 65; Also, you may transfer your home to the above, as well as
- Your child under 21; and

- Your child who has lived in the home for more than 2 years, providing care to you to keep you out of the nursing home.

One of our asset protect planning techniques used for single persons is the "Gift and Return". With this technique we can save approximately 50% of your assets. We have used the "Gift and Return" asset protection strategy successfully for a number of our clients. Basically, if you have $100,000 in assets, in lieu of giving the $100,000 to the nursing home (10 months x $10,000 per month = $100,000), we can save approximately $50,000. I feel it is better in your pocket rather than in the nursing homes pocket. As stated, Medicare and Medicaid do not pay for dental work, hearing aids, and eye glasses etc. So if you need any of these items, who will pay for them? You are only allowed less than $2,500 in assets, and all of your income, Social Security, pensions go to the nursing home, less your personal needs allowance of $77 (2016). Hearing aids are approximately over $4,000 – who will pay for this? So how is your quality of life, if you cannot see or hear properly because you cannot afford to pay for these items? We had client in the nursing home, and we performed the Gift and Return asset protection technique. We saved money for him. He was so grateful, as we purchased a television and new glasses for him. Also, with the money saved he was able to afford cable TV. He lived for a few years, and his enjoyment for the last remaining years was watching Animal Planet. If we had not saved these assets he would not have had a television, no glasses or been able to watch Animal Planet. How would his quality of life been without us saving some of his assets?

U. UNDUE INFLUENCE

The Maryland Attorney General's Office can help you with your consumer complaints, if you believe you have been defrauded by a business or door-to-door salesperson, illegally harassed by an unscrupulous debt collector, or victimized in deceptive sales practices by a home improvement contractor or mail order business. The Maryland Attorney General's Office investigates consumer complaints. The Maryland General's Office's telephone number is 1-888-743-0023, and their web address is www.oag.state.md.us.

Suggestions for Resolving Complaints

The Maryland Attorney General publishes consumer protection booklets. Some suggestions if you plan to resolve a complaint yourself:

- Decide the specific complaint you wish to make;
- Have a clear statement of the specific action you want the person or business to take to remedy your complaint;
- Proceed without delay;
- If you are making the complaint in person, take along the purchase receipt, any guaranty or warranty, if possible, the product;
- Be assertive! If you are told by a salesperson or company representative that they cannot deal with your complaint, ask for a higher authority;

- If you complain by mail, give the brand name, model number, size, color and other details needed for identifying the product. Include in your letter a specific explanation of the circumstances surrounding your complaint; and
- Keep copies of your letter and all correspondence you receive. If you return the product, be sure to insure it.

If you are unable to resolve your consumer complaint, you should contact the Maryland Attorney General's office or a consumer affairs attorney.

Avoiding Scams

The Maryland Attorney General's Office published the "A Consumer Guide for Seniors" a booklet that can help you to avoid scams and frauds. The booklet reiterates the phrase "If it sounds too good to be true, it probably is," and points out that scam artists typically use the "nice guy" approach. It also states that con artists often use words or expressions including:

- "Cash Only" – Why is it necessary for a proposed transaction? Why not a check or credit card?
- "Secret Plans" – why are you being asked not to tell anyone?
- "Get rich quick" – Any scheme should be carefully investigated.
- "Something for nothing" – A retired swindler once said that any time you are promised something for nothing, you usually get nothing.
- "Contests" – Make sure they aren't a hoax to draw you into a money-losing scheme.
- "Haste" - be wary of any pressure to act immediately or lose out.
- "Today only" – If something is worthwhile today, it is likely to be available tomorrow.
- "To good to be true" – Such a scheme is probably neither good nor true.
- "Last Chance" – If it is a chance worth taking, why is it offered on such short notice?

- "Left-over material" – Left-over materials might also be stolen or defective.

If you are unable to obtain the relief that you expected from the Consumer Protection Division of the Maryland Attorney General's Office, you should promptly seek legal advice from a qualified, Consumer affair's attorney, because there are strict time limits in which you must pursue any legal actions for fraud.

Charitable Organizations

Senior citizens who are solicited by charitable organizations can call the Charitable Organizations Division of the Maryland Secretary of State's Office at 1-800-825-4510 to find out if the organizations are registered to solicit contributions; how much income the organizations received; how much the organizations spend on programs, services, administration and fundraising. Seniors can also call the toll free number with any complaints they have about organizations which have solicited funds from them. Remember; call before you write the check.

Some precautions when you are called for donations:

- Ask for written information, including the charity's name, address and telephone number;
- Ask for identification; if the solicitor refuses, hang up;
- Call the charity to check whether they are aware of the solicitation. If they are not responsible, you should report the call to your local police department so they can investigate the potential for fraud;
- Watch out for organizational names which sound like established charities; some phony groups use titles that closely resemble respected legitimate organizations;
- Know that "tax-exempt" is not the same as "tax-deductible." The exemption refers to the organization but your contribution may or may not be tax deductible, and if that is important to you, ask for a receipt for the amount of your contribution;

- Be skeptical if someone thanks you for a pledge you do not remember making. Keep records and check them; and
- Refuse high pressure appeals. No legitimate organization should pressure you for your gift.

Mail Fraud

Mail fraud is illegal but it nevertheless remains a perfect means for a con artist to try to trick you. Do not respond to sweepstakes or contests that ask for money or your credit card number. For additional information on mail fraud, write to Criminal Investigations Service Center, Attn: Mail Fraud, 222 S. Riverside Plaza, Suite 1250, Chicago, IL 60606-6100 or call your local postmaster. If you think you are a victim of mail fraud, you can write or visit the postal service website at www.usps.com and submit a Mail Fraud Report.

Telemarketing

Telemarketing is another method commonly used to get your personal information such as credit card numbers, checking account numbers, Social Security number, driver's license number, etc. Do not give out this information unless you placed the call yourself to a well-known, reputable company. Other tips include:

- Never pay for a prize over the phone;
- Never allow a caller to pressure you into acting immediately;
- Never agree to any offer until you have seen it in writing; and
- The law prohibits telemarketers from calling consumers who have stated they do not want to be called.

Do Not Call Lists

Under this law, those who telemarket in Maryland, with some major exceptions, such as charities and political groups, are required to check their own lists on quarterly basis, to monitor who they may not call. Call registry online or telephone 1-888-382-1222.

Enforcement: If you believe a telemarketer is violating the law, you can file a complaint on line or by telephone at the above number or Internet address. There are no first tries, every violation should be reported.

Prerecorded calls are more problematical but a complaint can be filed with the FCC by calling 1-888-225-5322; online at www.fcc.gov/cbg/complaints.html, or by letter to the FCC Consumer and Governmental Affairs Bureau, Consumer Inquiries and Complaints Division, 445 12th Street, S.W. Washington, DC 20554. Prerecorded calls are illegal if made to residential phone lines. Exceptions include calls from tax-exempt nonprofits or from companies with which you already have an established business relationship.

Online Scms

On-line scams also are abundant in today's age of the internet. For the most part, the same rules apply so beware of being misled. For additional information about on-line scams, contact the National Fraud Information Center, Consumer Assistance Service at 1-800-876-7060 or visit their website at www.fraud.org.

Resources

The U.S. General Services Administration Consumer Information Center publishes a comprehensive "Consumer's Resource Handbook" which is available by writing the Consumer Information Center, Pueblo, CO 81009 or accessing the CIC website at www.pueblo.gsa.gov.

This publication has two parts: "Buying Smart" contains general advice on shopping; information on how to shop for major items such as cars, credit or home improvement; and suggestions on how to complain effectively including a sample letter of complaint. The second part is a "Consumer Association Directory" with lists of offices of consumer organizations, corporations, trade associations and government agencies at all levels.

Where to Get Help

To report suspected financial exploitation of a vulnerable adult, call the Maryland Department of Human Resources at 1-800-917-7383 Monday through Friday 8:00 a.m. to 5:00 p.m. The Department will contact Adult Protective Services in the appropriate county, which will investigate. You can make such a call completely anonymously. If you choose to give your identity, your identity will still be kept confidential.

V. VEHICLES

For many, driving is a source of independence and self-esteem. The vehicle is the only transportation for most of us. It allows us to operate on our own schedules, get to the doctor's office, get groceries, pick up the grandkids from school, and participate in all types of recreational activities. To maintain your standard of driving, however, you need to be aware of how physical changes associated with aging can ultimately affect your ability to drive.

Often, as we age, our eyesight and reactions change. Does driving make you feel nervous or overwhelmed? Do you feel confused by traffic signs? Do you take medication that makes you drowsy? Do you get dizzy; have seizures, or losses of consciousness? Do you react slowly to normal driving situations? If you said yes to any of the above questions, then these are some warning signs of unsafe driving.

No one wants to stop driving and give up control over the things they do in their life. However, a time may come when it may not be safe for you to drive. This is an issue that you and your family must confront. Discussing this with your family will allow your family members to appreciate that driving is very important to you. Also, it is extremely important that you talk to your physician about your driving ability. Your physician is one of the most, if not the most, influential person that you can talk to about your decision to stop driving.

In the State of Maryland, an individual may not drive or attempt to drive an automobile on any State highway without a driver's license.

The State of Maryland does not have an age-based suspension or revocation of a driving license. However, a vision test is required for renewal of your license.

The Motor Vehicle Administration ("MVA") may refer a driver to the Medical Advisory Board ("Board"), for an advisory opinion. This is done if the MVA has good cause to believe that the driving of a vehicle would be contrary to the public safety and welfare because of a known existing or suspected mental or physical disability. The Board is an advisory panel consisting of physicians and optometrists. The MVA, based on the Board's advisory opinion, may suspend, revoke, refuse to issue or renew the license if the licensee is unfit, unsafe, habitually reckless or negligent.

Once the MVA receives a referral, the driver in question is notified that they must appear for an examination. Failure to do so may lead to an automatic suspension of your license. At the examination review, the medical advisory board may perform tests.

Remember, driving is a privilege in the State of Maryland. The State can and will suspend or revoke your license if you are unfit to drive. Additionally, police officers have the right to stop your vehicle if they have probable cause because they suspect you of reckless or negligent driving. You may then have to appear in Court or in a MVA hearing regarding your driving ability.

To maintain your high standard of driving, you need to be aware of how your body changes as you age. Changes to vision, peripheral vision, depth perception, night vision, clarity of vision, reaction times, medications and mobility can interfere with your driving performance. These changes can lead to inappropriate driving speeds, failing to observe and follow signals, poor judgment of distances and speeds of other areas, frustration, confusion, getting lost in familiar areas, weaving in and out of traffic lanes, and near misses or accidents. Therefore, you may benefit from a driver refresher course before functional decline presents problems. Mature driver courses are offered by a variety of organizations i.e., AARP Driver Safety program. This refresher course may even lead to a discount in your insurance.

When you do have to drive, remember these safe driving tips:

- Try to avoid left turns. If possible, make several right turns to get where you want.
- Always slow down and signal, in advance of your turn.
- Allow plenty of time and room to make your turn.
- Keep a safe distance between you and the vehicle ahead.
- Sit high in your seat.
- Avoid driving at dawn, dusk, rush hour and at night.
- Always wear your current prescription glasses.

At some point you may need to stop driving for your safety and the safety of others on the road. You may come to this decision yourself, or by the recommendation of the doctor, or MVA. When you or someone close to you retires from driving, there are several things you can do to make it easier for you and your family.

Create a transportation plan:

- Come up with a list of names and telephone numbers - who are willing to give rides.
- Have handy the phone numbers of taxi cabs / shuttle bus services.
- Contact the Department of Aging
- Arrange to have groceries delivered.
- Order medications by mail.
- Shop by catalogs.

Should you have to give up your vehicle, look on the bright side of things. You will no longer have to pay the cost of fuel, vehicle maintenance, insurance, vehicle payments, etc. which may result in savings to you.

Driving issues are complex, especially with the dependence of the vehicle in our society today and limited public transportation in many areas or communities. However, failure to act responsibly may force the State of Maryland to act on your behalf.

W. WILL

A Will is an important legal document and is the foundation of most estate plans. A Will specifies how your property is distributed, when you die. Additionally, a Will can designate who will be the Guardian of your minor children if you and the other child's parent are deceased.

Every person should have a Will. Otherwise, the State of Maryland has a Will for you as you have died intestate (died without a Will). Thus, your property will be distributed according to the State of Maryland's Laws, which may or may not be your desire.

The requirements for a valid will:

- Over 18;
- Be of sound mind;
- Typewritten;
- Distribution of property;
- Appoints a Personal Representative;
- Dated;
- Witnessed by two independent people.

In your Will, you should name a Personal Representative (Executor) who manages your estate. The functions of the Personal Representative is to deal with the probate court i.e. filing forms; collect and appraise your assets; pay your debts taxes; and distribute your assets to your specified beneficiaries.

With a Will, all of you property will pass through probate, unless the property has been titled in joint tenancy, a living revocable trust, payable of death, or having a named beneficiary.

As previously discussed, I recommend a Revocable Trust over a Will to avoid Probate. A revocable living trust ("trust") is an effective approach to transfer property at your death and thus avoid probate. Basically, a trust is an estate planning document which allows an individual to direct another person (the trustee) to manage property during the individual's life and to distribute property upon the individual's death, according to the individual's specific wishes. Unlike a Will, a trust is not probated.

We are always asked when you should review your estate planning documents. A good rule of thumb is to review your documents every two to three years. Do you still agree with the arrangements you made previously i.e. appointing the Trustee or Personal Representative, distribution of your property? Update your documents if circumstances have changed i.e. marriage, divorce, death, birth, inherited money or won the lotto.

X. X OUT YOUR ISSUES

There are often legal issues which arise as we age. There may be questions regarding your healthcare, making financial decisions, to how your property should pass at your death.

Following is a list of some of the reasons why it's important to deal with an attorney skilled in helping families:

- **It's important to deal with an attorney who concentrates his or her practice on these types of issues.** Helping families through this difficult time takes a special set of skills. Not only is it important to have an attorney who understands the technical part of the law, but it's also critical to have an attorney who understands the emotional aspects. You want someone you will be comfortable with, and someone who has provided the services to countless families going through the same issues you and your family face now.
- **The attorney's staff must also be well-trained.** While it's important to deal with an attorney who is sensitive and understands the issues you're facing...it's also crucial to deal with an attorney whose practice is geared toward helping you and your loved ones. Plus it's important that the attorney's staff also understands all of the challenges you are facing.
- **You want an attorney who understands the government programs that are available to you.** In this day and age, it's difficult for any professional to know all there's to know about any given topic. That's especially true when it comes to issues of government benefits i.e. Medicare and Medicaid.

It's important that you deal with an attorney who works frequently in this area and who is used to dealing with the State. You need an attorney who knows how to help you and your family.

- **It's important to deal with an attorney who knows how to help you to protect your life's savings.** No matter the size of your estate, you worked hard to earn it. It's important to you and it's important to your family that you pass along as much of it as possible. When selecting an attorney, be sure that he or she is knowledgeable on how to help you arrange things so that you receive the care you need and so that your assets will be preserved for your family to the greatest extent allowed by the law.
- **How to avoid probate** - For many clients, one of the most important concerns in the event of their death is that they want their estate to pass to their loved ones without going through probate. There are many ways to accomplish this, ranging from simple beneficiary designations to gifting strategies to trust planning and so on. It is important that you deal with an attorney who understands the various ways that property passes and who can show you how to arrange your estate to avoid probate.
- **It is important to work with an attorney who knows the value of a dollar.** One of the biggest gripes people have in dealing with legal professionals is that they feel like they are "on the clock" and will be charged extra for every question they ask or every time they pick up the phone. Where possible, you should consider an attorney who works on a flat fee basis. Ideally, you want someone who will tell you to the penny exactly what will be involved and what the cost will be. That way you can be a smart consumer and get the most for your dollar, while making sure that things are handled in the most appropriate manner.

All of these are reasons why it is important to deal with someone who practices in this important area of the law and who has sensitivity to the needs of clients and their families. If you would like an initial consultation with an attorney who has helped hundreds of local families deal with these types of issues, then call David Wingate at The Elder Law Office of David Wingate, LLC.

Consultation

If you or a loved one has dementia, Parkinson disease, concerned about the well-being of your family or simply aging, the ability to make financial and healthcare decisions may decrease over time, there are steps you can take right now to protect yourself, your family, and your assets.

Fortunately, proper planning will assure that things are handled according to your wishes and that you've taken the best steps possible to protect your loved ones and to protect your family.

Call now to discuss your concerns with an attorney who understands the aging process and the special challenges a life threatening illness can present.

Y. YOUNG CHILDREN

If you die, and desire to leave some or all of assets to your minor children (under 18) you have three ways of doing it:

- Uniform Transfers to Minors Act;
- Trust; and
- Guardianship.

Under the Uniform Transfers to Minor Act ("UTMA"), you identify the property and the minor you are bequeathing it to. You appoint a custodian who is responsible for managing the property until the child, at the designated ages, receives the property. The custodian has the responsibility for administering and using the property in the child's interest.

Another way to manage a child's inheritance is through a trust. With the trust, you leave property in the trust for the child's benefit until they reach a certain age. A trust is a legal document, where a Trustee has the responsibility for managing the property, for the child's interest. The Trustee's powers are specified in the trust documents.

Usually, the trustee may use the trust property for the child's education, medical needs and maintenance, until the child becomes of age.

If you name a Guardian of the Property for your minor child, your property will have to go through the probate process. Additionally, the Guardian of the property is subject to court oversite, with reports and strict guidelines on how they can spend the funds. Also, the Guardianship will end when the child reaches the age of 18.

Z. IS THE END

Elder Law is used by the Legal profession to focus on the rights of seniors be it estate planning financial and asset protection planning, healthcare, housing and government programs.

Additionally, many people think estate planning is only for the wealthy. Nothing is more far from the truth. If you can own property you need to have a plan to avoid disputes amongst your children and your relatives.

This book is designed to provide you with general information. I hope that after reading this book you can make appropriate choices for you and your loved ones. Clearly, no book can cover all the issues of elder law and estate planning but I hope this book offers some basic information that can help you with your individual needs.

The information provided in this book is for informational purposes only and is not offered for and does not constitute legal advice or legal opinion, tax and financial planning or any specific fact or issues.

ABOUT DAVID WINGATE

David Wingate is the President of the Elder Law Office of David Wingate, LLC. Mr. Wingate's professional practice is devoted to representing his clients through the aging process. He has served on Boards for local and national organizations and charities. Additionally, he is a member of the National Academy of Elder Law Attorneys and the Maryland State Bar – Elder Law and Estate Planning sections. Mr. Wingate has received the honor of being voted, by his peers, as the #1 Elder Law Attorney, in his community. Also, he has written a book called "As You Age" and written numerous articles on a variety of aging topics, and is a frequent speaker on aging issues for the Alzheimer Association, AARP, radio and television.

www.ingramcontent.com/pod-product-compliance
Lightning Source LLC
Chambersburg PA
CBHW022115170526
45157CB00004B/1656